THE
LONGEST
KICK

ELAYNE REISS-WEIMANN
RITA FRIEDMAN

NEW DIMENSIONS IN EDUCATION, INC.
50 EXECUTIVE BLVD.
ELMSFORD, NY 10523

Printed in U.S.A.

ISBN 0-89796-990-1

1 2 3 4 5 6 7 9 0 SPC SPC 8 9 3 2 1 0 9   12402

Every Sunday some people go to Klanksville
to watch a football game.
However, every Sunday even more people go
to Letter People Land to listen to a football story.
This is the football story.

1

One day a new Letter Person
comes to Letter People Land.
"I am Mr. K," he says.
"Sometimes I'm called Kicking K."
"I hope you are careful not to kick anyone,"
says the mayor.
"I never kick anything but a ball," smiles Mr. K.
"Right now I am practicing kicking footballs."

The mayor shows Mr. K a field where he may kick.
The field is at the bottom of a high hill.
"What is on the other side of the hill?" asks Mr. K.
"The town of Klanksville," answers the mayor.
"Klanksville!" repeats Mr. K, very excited.

"I've heard of Klanksville," says Mr. K.
"Klanksville has a famous football team.
Maybe someday I can be the team kicker."
"Can you kick far?" asks the mayor.
"Not yet," says Mr. K,
"but I will keep practicing."

Every day Mr. K goes to the field to practice kicking.
He practices and practices,
but he cannot kick the ball far.
People come to watch Mr. K kick.
Day after day Mr. K asks,
"Do you think I am good enough to be the kicker
for the Klanksville team?"
"We're sorry, Mr. K," they answer.
"You do not kick the ball very far."
"I will keep trying," says Mr. K.

One day there is a terrible storm
in Letter People Land.
The wind blows and blows.
It blows down trees.
It rains and rains.
The rain floods the streets.
It is impossible to drive.
The telephones do not work.
Letter People Land is in trouble.

11

The people meet at the Town Hall.
"We need help," says the mayor.
"I have tried to reach Klanksville,
but there is no way to reach them."
Suddenly, Mr. K rushes in carrying a large sack.
"I have a way to reach Klanksville," he says.
"Follow me!"

Mr. K and the people row boats
through the flooded streets.
Luckily, the wind and rain have stopped.
Mr. K and the people row to the practice field.
"Mr. K," says the mayor,
"we don't have time to watch you kick.
We must find a way to reach Klanksville."
"I will show you the way," says Mr. K proudly.

15

Mr. K asks everyone to climb to the top of the hill.

"Now look carefully," says Mr. K.

"Far, far away you can see Klanksville."

"Seeing Klanksville will not help us," says the mayor.

"We must get a message to the town."

"I have a way to do it," says Mr. K.

He takes a red football out of the sack.

17

Mr. K lifts the red football.

Everyone reads, "Send help to Letter People Land."

"This sack is filled with red footballs," says Mr. K.

"I painted the same message on each football."

"Mr. K," says the mayor,

"what are we going to do with a sack of footballs?"

"I will kick and kick," answers Mr. K.

"One football will surely reach Klanksville."

Everyone laughs and laughs.

Mr. K looks very sad.

"We did not mean to hurt your feelings,"
says the mayor.

"However, it is impossible for anyone to kick a football
as far as Klanksville."

"Sometimes, if you keep trying, anything is possible,"
says Mr. K.

"Please let me try."

"Try Mr. K! Try Mr. K!" shout all the people.

Mr. K kicks a red football.

Everyone cheers.

Alas, the football does not go very far.

Mr. K takes another football out of the sack.

He kicks it.

This football does not go very far either.

Mr. K kicks and kicks and kicks.

He cannot kick a football to Klanksville.

Suddenly, a strong wind starts blowing.

"We must return to the Town Hall," says the mayor.

"Wait!" says Mr. K.

"This is the last football.

Please let me kick it.

I will try harder than I have ever tried before."

Everyone waits.

Mr. K kicks the ball high into the air.

All at once, the wind blows stronger
than it has ever blown before.
The wind lifts up the red football.
The football floats on and on with the wind.
Everyone cheers and cheers.
Soon the football is out of sight.

Everyone returns to the Town Hall.

"Mr. K," says the mayor,

"the football will probably never reach Klanksville.

However, we are very proud of you.

You tried very hard to help us."

Suddenly, everyone hears loud noises.

"I hear sirens and horns," says Mr. K.

Everyone rushes outside.

The Klanksville fire engines and police cars are arriving.

"How did Klanksville know we needed help?"

wonders the mayor.

Suddenly, the mayor sees the Klanksville chief of police.

She is holding a

red

football!